MAP MY
SCHOOL

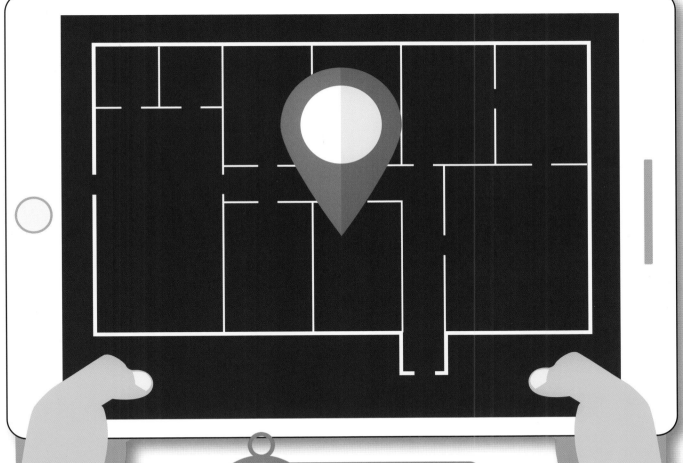

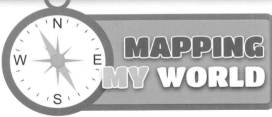

MAPPING
MY WORLD

CRABTREE
PUBLISHING COMPANY
WWW.CRABTREEBOOKS.COM

Published in Canada
Crabtree Publishing
616 Welland Avenue
St. Catharines, ON
L2M 5V6

Published in the United States
Crabtree Publishing
PMB 59051
350 Fifth Ave, 59th Floor
New York, NY 10118

Published in 2019 by Crabtree Publishing Company

First Published by Book Life in 2018
Copyright © 2018 Book Life

Author: Harriet Brundle

Editors: Kirsty Holmes, Kathy Middleton

Design: Matt Rumbelow

Proofreader: Janine Deschenes

Prepress technician: Tammy McGarr

Print coordinator: Katharine Berti

All facts, statistics, web addresses, and URLs in this book were verified as valid and accurate at time of writing. No responsibility for any changes to external websites or references can be accepted by either the author or publisher.

Photographs

Images are courtesy of Shutterstock.com. With thanks to Getty Images, Thinkstock Photo and iStockphoto With thanks to 2 – 7 pips. 3 – Art Alex. 5 – fad82. 6 – Sentavio. 7: Peter, Happy Art. 8 – keri_aa. 9 – Art Alex. 10: t – ProStockStudio,11 – 7 pips. 13: ProStockStudio, Boguslaw Mazur, Artem Kulturen. 14 – Lorelyn Medina. 15: outer – Rainer Lesniewski, inner – Rainer Lesniewski. 16 – Bardocz Peter. 17 – Susse_n_2. 18 – Macrovector. 19 – turbodesign. 20 – YAZZIK. 21 – Sergii88. 22: l – Dark ink, c – Neda Sadreddin, r – stickerama. 23 – Ciripasca, Dr Project.

Printed in the U.S.A./082018/CG20180601

Library and Archives Canada Cataloguing in Publication

Brundle, Harriet, author
      Map my school / Harriet Brundle.

(Mapping my world)
Includes index.
Issued in print and electronic formats.
ISBN 978-0-7787-5000-0 (hardcover).--
ISBN 978-0-7787-5004-8 (softcover).--
ISBN 978-1-4271-2129-5 (HTML)

      1. Cartography--Juvenile literature. 2. Maps--Juvenile literature.
I. Title.

GA105.6.B795 2018   j526   C2018-902378-3
                                         C2018-902379-1

Library of Congress Cataloging-in-Publication Data

Names: Brundle, Harriet, author.
Title: Map my school / Harriet Brundle.
Description: New York, New York : Crabtree Publishing, 2019. |
  Series: Mapping my world | Includes index.
Identifiers: LCCN 2018021325 (print) | LCCN 2018027505 (ebook) |
  ISBN 9781427121295 (Electronic) |
  ISBN 9780778750000 (hardcover) |
  ISBN 9780778750048 (pbk.)
Subjects: LCSH: Cartography--Juvenile literature. | Map reading--Juvenile
  literature. | Floor plans--Juvenile literature. | Building sites--Juvenile
  literature. | Schools--Design and construction--Juvenile literature. |
  School buildings--Design and construction--Juvenile literature.
Classification: LCC GA105.6 (ebook) | LCC GA105.6 .B794 2019 (print) |
  DDC 526--dc23
LC record available at https://lccn.loc.gov/2018021325

CONTENTS

Words that look like this can be found in the glossary on page 24.

WHAT IS A MAP?

A map is a picture that gives us information about an area. Maps can show us a lot of different things. A map can show streets, stores, or even rooms inside a building.

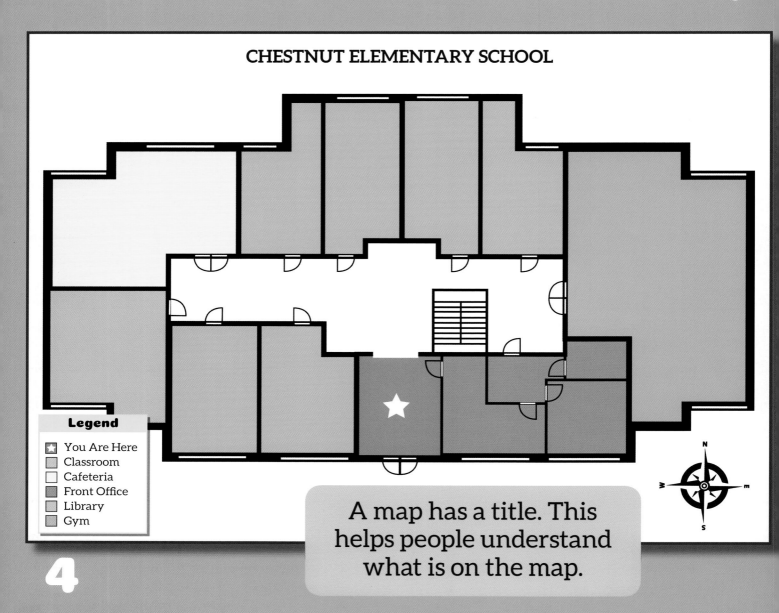

CHESTNUT ELEMENTARY SCHOOL

Legend
- ⭐ You Are Here
- Classroom
- Cafeteria
- Front Office
- Library
- Gym

A map has a title. This helps people understand what is on the map.

Some maps are printed on paper. Some maps are viewed on screens. These are called **digital** maps.

USING A MAP

It is hard to see all of an area or inside every room in a building from where you are standing. A map gives you a "bird's-eye view" of an entire area. This means the map shows you what a bird could see looking down from high above.

Maps can help you see how to get from one place to another.

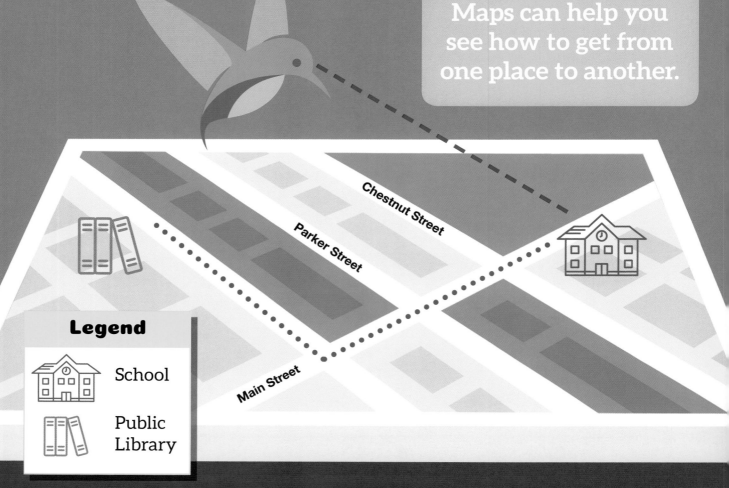

Legend

School

Public Library

Compass Rose

A map usually has a **compass rose** in the corner. The points on a compass rose are marked with the letters N, E, W, and S. They show you which direction is north, south, east, or west.

LEGEND

Maps show where things are by using symbols and colors. Symbols are pictures that stand for other things. A map has a list called a legend that shows what the symbols and colors stand for. The legend usually appears in a corner of the map.

You might see a symbol like this to show where a school is on a map.

Legend

School   House

8

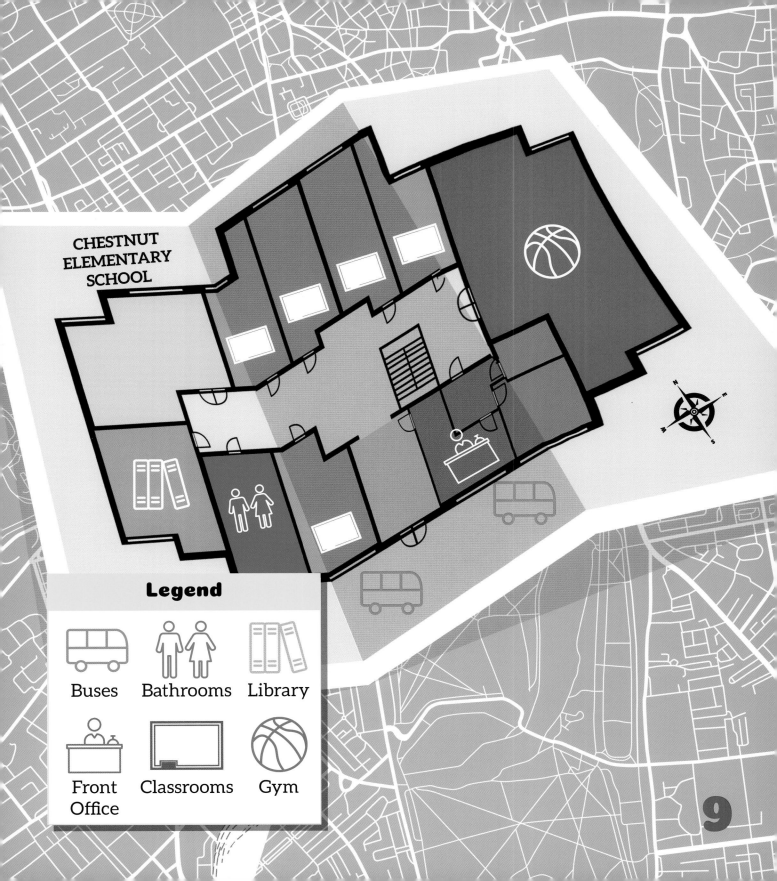

CHESTNUT ELEMENTARY SCHOOL

Legend

Buses	Bathrooms	Library
Front Office	Classrooms	Gym

9

SCALE

A building is too big to show on a map at its real size. Everything on a map is made smaller by the same amount so it will fit on the paper or a screen. The amount it has been shrunk is called the scale.

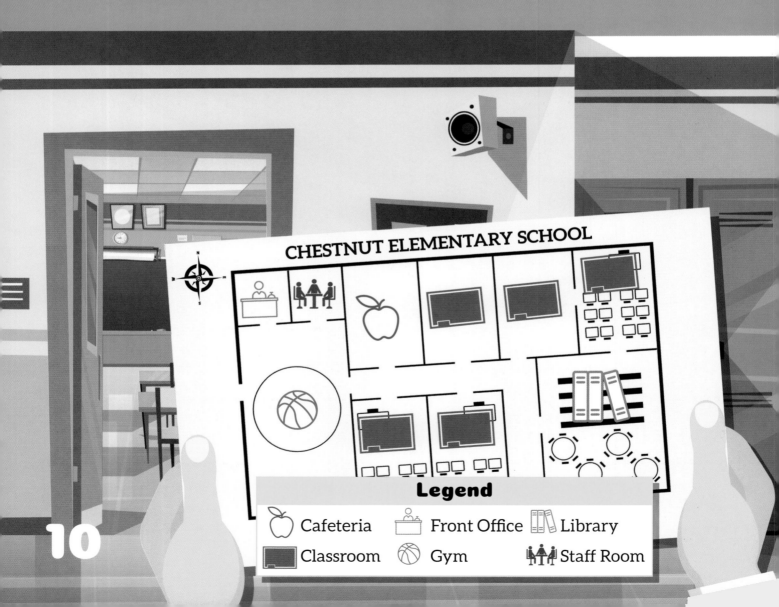

CHESTNUT ELEMENTARY SCHOOL

Legend

Cafeteria Front Office Library

Classroom Gym Staff Room

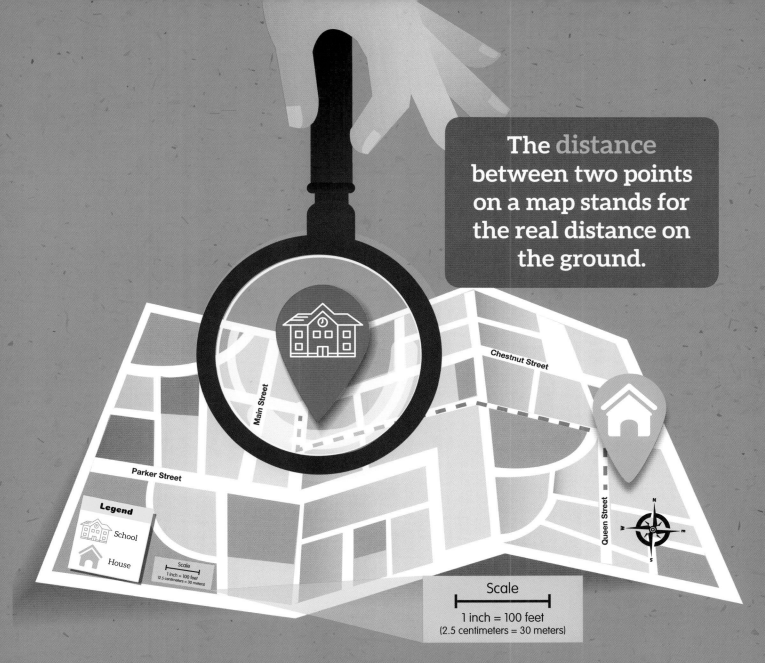

Chestnut Street

Main Street

Parker Street

Queen Street

Legend

School

House

Scale
1 inch = 100 feet
(2.5 centimeters = 30 meters)

Scale

1 inch = 100 feet
(2.5 centimeters = 30 meters)

N
W E
S

The scale is found near the legend. You can use the scale on a map to figure out distance on the ground. To find the real distance between your home and school, measure the distance on the map with a ruler. Then multiply that number by the scale.

11

DIFFERENT MAPS

We use different kinds of maps for different reasons.

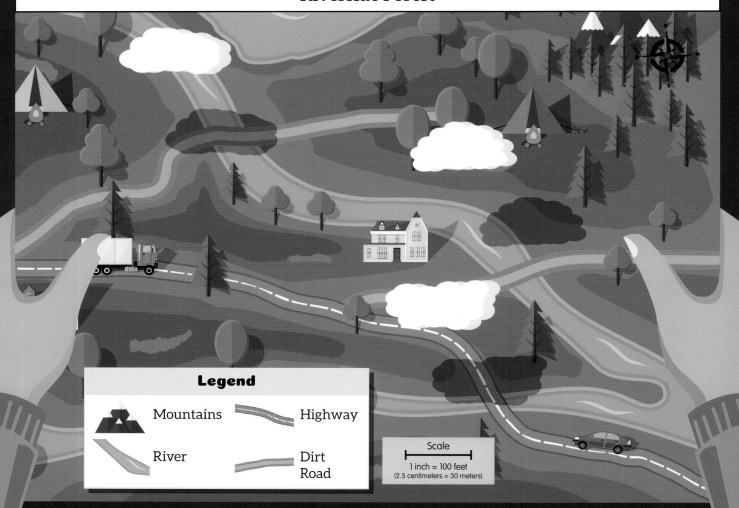

Riverside Forest

Legend

Mountains

River

Highway

Dirt Road

Scale
1 inch = 100 feet
(2.5 centimeters = 30 meters)

Physical maps show the **landforms** in an area. Landforms are the shapes of the land, such as mountains or rivers.

Sometimes you need to find your way inside a building. A map of a building, such as a school, shows the layout of the rooms and floors.

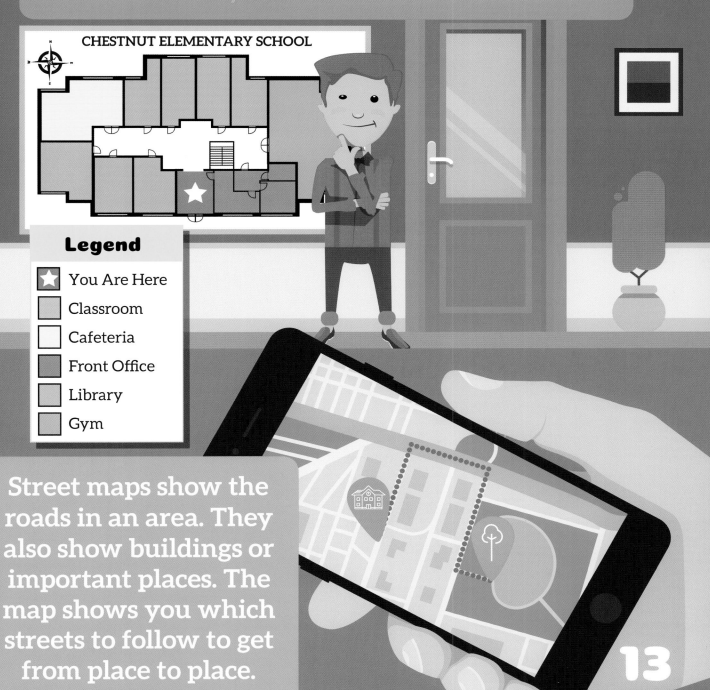

CHESTNUT ELEMENTARY SCHOOL

Legend

⭐ You Are Here

▢ Classroom

▢ Cafeteria

▢ Front Office

▢ Library

▢ Gym

Street maps show the roads in an area. They also show buildings or important places. The map shows you which streets to follow to get from place to place.

13

WHO USES A SCHOOL MAP?

Parents and caregivers often don't know their way around a school as well as their children do. Neither do children or teachers from other schools who may be coming for a sports or math competition.

A school map can help visitors find out how to get to the gym or the classroom they are looking for.

If you were starting at a new school, a map could help you find your way around.

CHESTNUT ELEMENTARY SCHOOL

Legend

★ You Are Here
▢ Classroom
▢ Cafeteria
▢ Front Office
▢ Library
▢ Gym

FLOOR PLANS

A map that shows the layout of a building is called a floor plan.

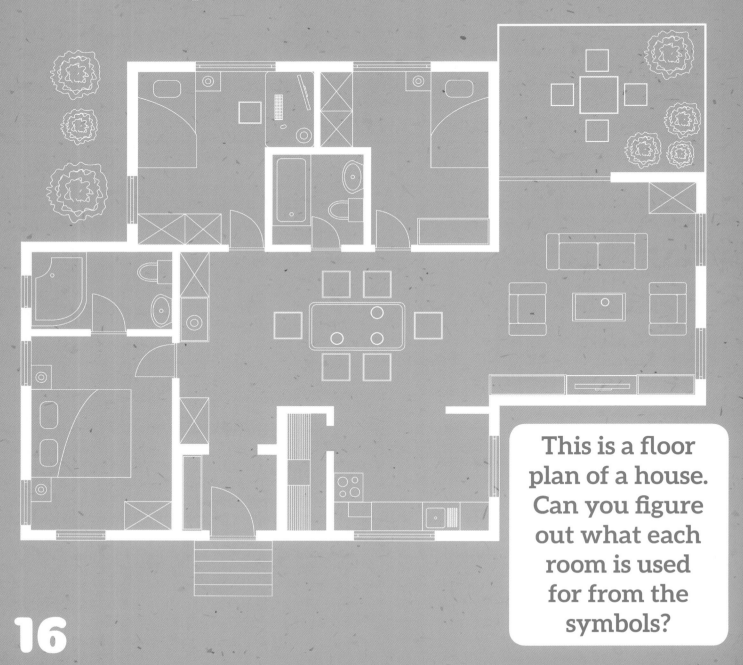

This is a floor plan of a house. Can you figure out what each room is used for from the symbols?

16

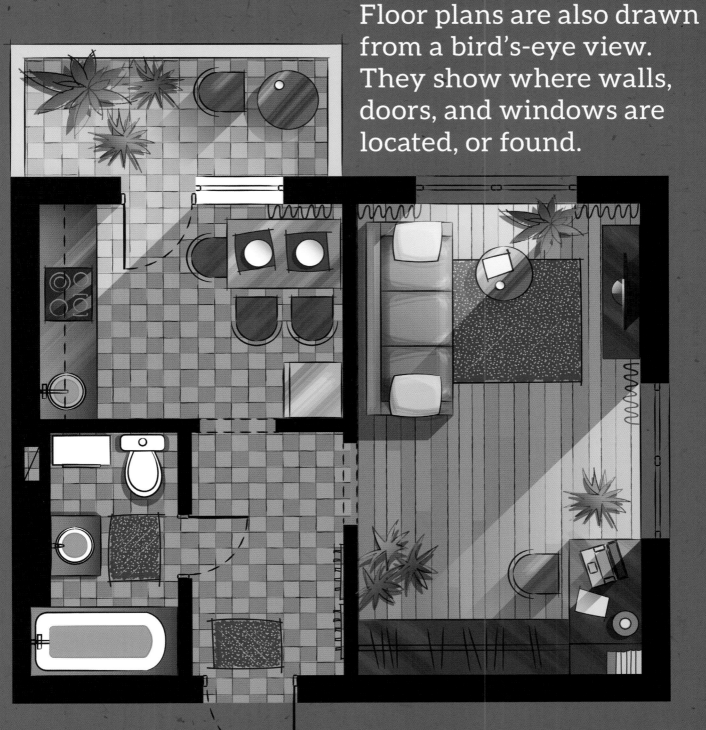

Floor plans are also drawn from a bird's-eye view. They show where walls, doors, and windows are located, or found.

17

MAPPING MY SCHOOL

STEP 1 – LIST IMPORTANT AREAS

The first step to mapping your school is to make a list of all the important areas. In a school, these could include classrooms, bathrooms, and the library. Don't forget hallways and stairs. Can you think of more important areas?

STEP 2 – CREATE A LEGEND

Next, you need to create a legend with symbols for each important area.

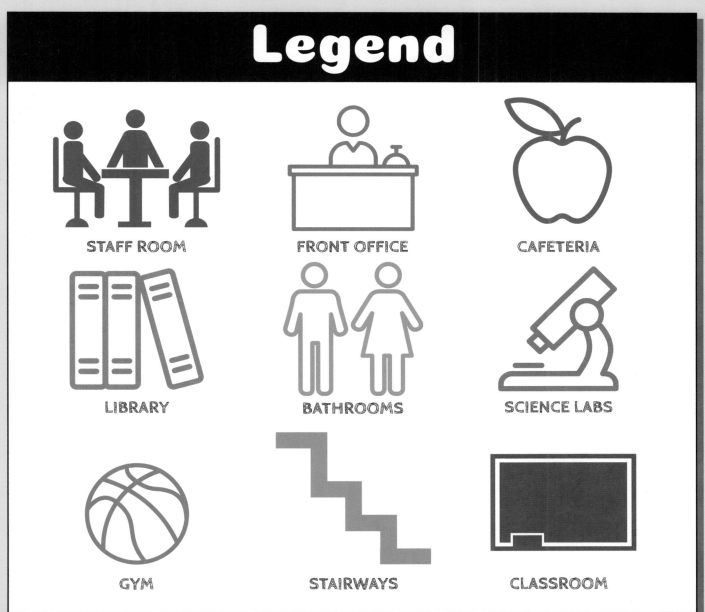

Legend

STAFF ROOM

FRONT OFFICE

CAFETERIA

LIBRARY

BATHROOMS

SCIENCE LABS

GYM

STAIRWAYS

CLASSROOM

STEP 3 – DRAW YOUR FLOOR PLAN

Imagine you could look down at your school from above. Start by drawing the shape of the building.

Is your school built in a square shape like this?

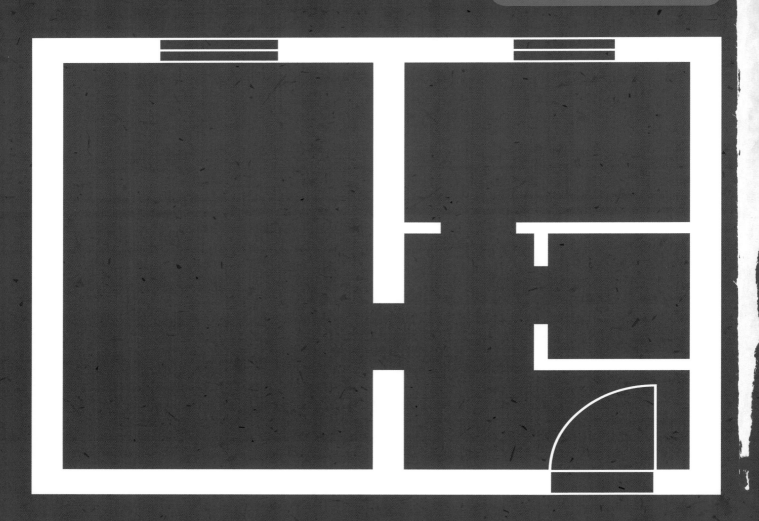

STEP 4 – ADD THE DETAILS

Draw the walls of the rooms and hallways. Add symbols from your legend to show what each room is used for. You can even add furniture. If your school has more than one floor, make a floor plan for each floor.

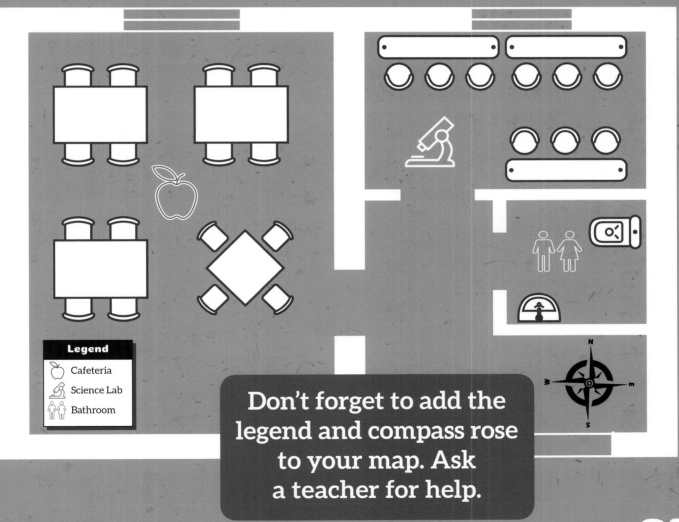

Legend
🍎 Cafeteria
🔬 Science Lab
🚻 Bathroom

Don't forget to add the legend and compass rose to your map. Ask a teacher for help.

MAP ACTIVITY
GIVE DIRECTIONS TO A NEW STUDENT AT YOUR SCHOOL

Now that you have drawn a school map, imagine that you have to tell a new student how to get from one place to another.

Give directions such as "Go north," or "Turn left," or "Go past."

You could try giving the new student directions from the front office to the gym. Then tell them how to get from the gym to a certain classroom. Draw the paths they should follow in colored pencil on the map.

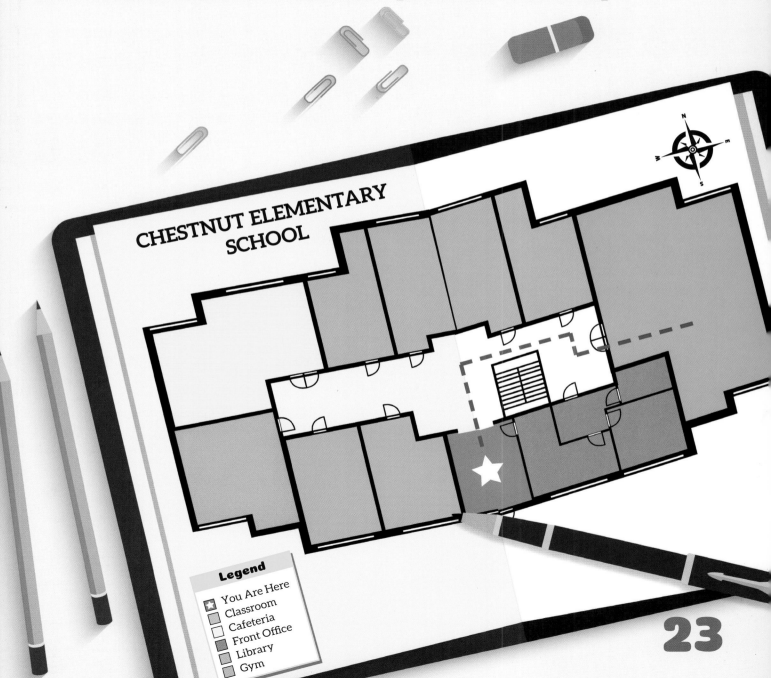

CHESTNUT ELEMENTARY SCHOOL

Legend
- ⭐ You Are Here
- Classroom
- Cafeteria
- Front Office
- Library
- Gym

GLOSSARY AND INDEX

GLOSSARY

area A specific place, such as land

bird's-eye view Seeing or looking down on something from high above

compass rose A map part that shows which ways point north, south, east, and west

digital Display using electronic or computer technology

distance The space between two points

floor plan A drawing of all the rooms in a building from a bird's-eye view

landform Features on Earth's surface formed by nature, such as mountains

layout The way the parts of something are arranged

legend A map part that lists symbols and their meanings

physical Something you can see and touch

scale The amount by which everything on a map has been shrunk so it fits on a page or screen

symbols A shape or picture that stands for a building, place, or other object

INDEX